WESTERN
AUSTRALIA

Published in Australia by Gordon & Gotch Ltd.

First published in Great Britain 1984 by Colour Library Books Ltd.
© 1984 Illustrations and text: Colour Library Books Ltd.,
    Guildford, Surrey, England.
Display and text filmsetting by Acesetters Ltd.,
    Richmond, Surrey, England.
Colour separations by Llovet, Barcelona, Spain.
Printed and bound in Barcelona, Spain.
by JISA-RIEUSSET and EUROBINDER.
ISBN 0 86283 145 8

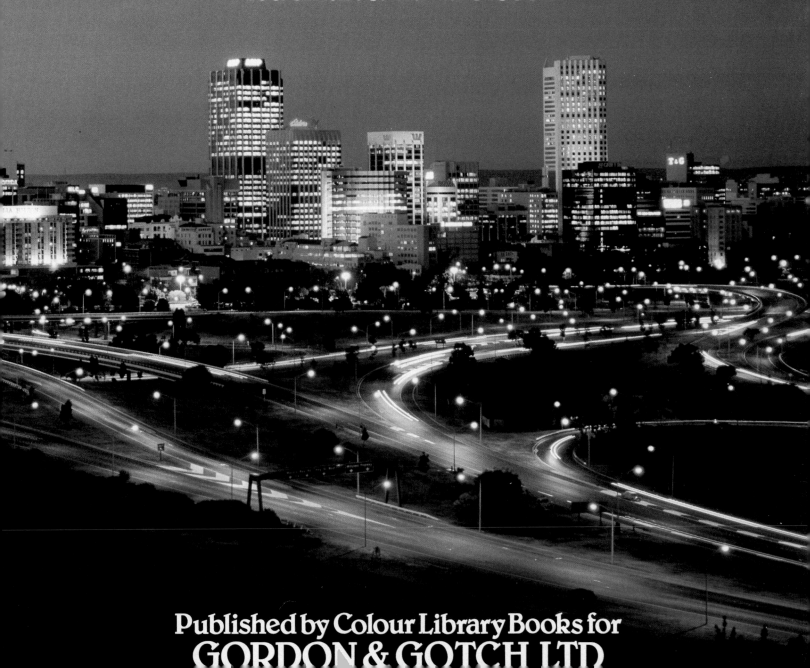

AUSTRALIA'S HERITAGE

WESTERN AUSTRALIA

Produced by
Ted Smart & David Gibbon

Published by Colour Library Books for
GORDON & GOTCH LTD

The sheer scale of Western Australia staggers the imagination. It covers more than two and a half million square kilometres and if its coastline were stretched out, it would reach two thirds of the way to London. The state has the longest straight line of railway track in the world, 483 kilometres across the Nullarbor Plain, and one of the world's greatest stock routes, the Canning, which runs for 1,600 kilometres across the Red Centre. Yet despite this vastness of area the population remains an amazingly low one and a quarter million.

The vast reaches of Western Australia were amongst the last on the continent to be explored and exploited, but they were by no means the last to be settled. In 1627, just twenty-two years after Willem Jansz first sighted the continent near Cape York, Pieter Nuyts sailed into Esperance Bay. Captain Nuyts was following the reports of several Dutch captains who had been swept off course while sailing from the Cape of Good Hope to Java and who told of a vast, unexplored landmass far to the south of Jansz's sighting. Nuyts sailed for 1,600 kilometres along the coast before returning home. Despite this early activity the Dutch soon lost interest and 'New Holland' slipped back into peaceful obscurity.

Nearly sixty years after Nuyts had quit the shores of *Terra Australis Incognita* a British rogue, by the name of William Dampier, touched the northeastern coast of New Holland in search of water and supplies. At that time Dampier was making a living by plundering ships in the South Seas. He was a pirate. But this did not stop him openly returning to Britain and calmly talking the Admiralty into financing him to return to the other side of the globe on a voyage of exploration. When he returned in 1699, Dampier charted the coast with remarkable accuracy and produced a report of great insight. Unfortunately, he had sailed along just about the worst two thousand kilometre stretch of coast in Australia – that around what is now Broome and Roebuck Bay – with the result that his report dismissed the land as unproductive and worthless.

It was nearly a century before anyone bothered to visit the western part of the landmass again. Even then the exploration added little to the knowledge gained by Nuyts and Dampier. In 1801, the British naval officer Matthew Flinders skirted the southern and western coasts of the continent, thus proving, once and for all, that New Holland, New South Wales and various other places were really one landmass. He suggested that the continent be named Australia and, in 1817, the British government gave the name official backing. By this time New South Wales had been a flourishing colony for some years, taking convicts and providing a stopover point for British ships.

In 1827, Captain Stirling explored the Swan River area and returned with such glowing reports that he was able to interest several capitalist adventurers in founding a new colony. The government at the time was worried that a foreign power might found a colony on the unclaimed western third of Australia as a challenge to British settlements on the continent. With the memories of the bloody and costly conflicts such rivalry had caused in India and America fresh in its mind, the British government approved the scheme.

Two years later Captain Stirling returned and, on June 17 1829, read out a proclamation declaring that the whole western third of Australia belonged to Britain and that he was to be the first Lieutenant Governor. Though he only had 150 settlers with him, James Stirling was not in the least daunted by the prospect of settling an area ten times the size of Britain. Fremantle was founded at the mouth of the Swan River, to act as a port, and a slight hill was named Perth and declared to be the capital city. Within two years the population had increased tenfold to 1,500 souls. Western Australia was thus one of the first colonies to be founded.

But once the initial settlement had taken place, and the diplomatic point had been made, the government lost interest and for decades the story of Western Australia was one of survival rather than prosperity. But despite the lack of investment and interest from home, the hardy Westerners managed to gain a living and modestly to increase their wealth and numbers. While the other colonies were gaining responsible self-government, Western Australia remained under direct Imperial control. In 1870, the colony gained a legislature which was partly elected and partly nominated by the Imperial government. Within twenty years this system had been replaced by fully responsible government and the famous John Forrest became premier.

The rather quiet life of the state was to change dramatically, though some would debate whether it was for the better, in 1893. On a certain day that year a "decent, bearded little man" from Ireland, by the name of Paddy Hannan, walked northeast from the little town of Coolgardie straight into the tales of legend. What Paddy found some thirty-odd kilometres into the outback was the dream and inspiration of thousands of his fellow countrymen. He found the fabled 'mother lode', a reef of gold-bearing rock so rich that the area became known as 'The Golden Mile'. This discovery brought prosperity to the desert and caused an explosive growth in the wealth and population of Western Australia. Paddy Hannan has, quite rightly, become almost a folk hero; Coolgardie and Kalgoorlie, which still mine the reef of gold, have remembered him in street names, the local beer is named after him and a statue of him sits outside the Town Hall distributing water to any passer-by.

Four years after Paddy Hannan's momentous discovery, Harold Lasseter returned from an expedition into the Petermann Ranges of the Red Centre. He had discovered a reef of gold ore even more fabulous than that found by Paddy. Unfortunately, by the time he had gathered together enough money to mount a return expedition, he had forgotten where the gold was and could not find it. Nobody else could either, and to this day 'Lasseter's Reef' remains a legend of the gold rush days.

The inevitable lure of gold brought to the area thousands of miners, together with barkeepers and store owners. Almost overnight the population of Coolgardie leapt to fifteen thousand and water became a great problem; there wasn't any. Some water could be distilled from the salt water of Lake Charlotte, but as the boom continued to gather strength it was clear that this was not enough. The hardy pioneers built a pipeline from the coast, 556 kilometres away. However, another popular way to make up for the lack of water was to drink beer. It is rumoured that at Boulder, near Kalgoorlie, there were "six pubs to the bloomin' acre", and they never shut. The hordes of shift workers that came in at all hours of the day kept the bars busy and the amount of beer consumed was truly phenomenal. It was here, out in the goldfields, that the Australian 'Digger' first took shape. The picture of a tough, self-reliant outdoorsman who is always ready to help his cobber, is the most popular image of the Australian in the world at large. Though today most Australians live in cities, the idea of the Digger persists, and has its roots in the Western Australian gold rushes.

The gold rush is gone, and there are many ghost towns to witness its passing, and even Coolgardie is now down to one thousand inhabitants, but mining is still an industry of great importance to the state. The mineral wealth of Western Australia is proving to be far greater than anyone could possibly have imagined; except perhaps Harold Lasseter. The deposits of iron ore, nickel, bauxite and, of course, gold that are being exploited in the state are truly vast, and more are being discovered every year. In the hills and mountains behind the coast around Port Hedland, towns such as Paraburdoo and Tom Price pour out the earth's natural wealth. Such is the volume of production from the area that new 'Pilbara ports' are being constructed along the state's northwestern coast. Ironically, one of these has been named Dampier, in honour of the British pirate who did so much to deter settlement in the area. It is not only ores that are found in the area; an important oil exploration project is in progress off the coast. Gas has long been a product of Yardarino, from where a 362 kilometre long pipeline runs to Pinjarra, far to the southwest.

The burning, desolate interior is not only famous for its mineral wealth and historic ghost towns of the gold rushes – some of the continent's most spectacular scenery can be found here. In the heart of the Pilbara mining area is Wittenoon, a region of dramatic canyons and gorges cut deep into the rock by the rivers of the area. The gorges continue to the south where the beauties of Yampire Gorge, Dales Gorge and the Fortescue Falls have prompted the Federal Government to create a National Park measuring some 120 kilometres long by 80 wide around the area. Some 400 kilometres to the east lies the even larger Rudall River National Park. Many of the rivers in the Australian outback only flow when there is enough rainfall; in other words very rarely. Even when they do run with water, their courses ensure that they never reach the sea. Descending from the mountains where the rain falls, the rivers flow out into the deserts of Australia, in the case of the Rudall across the Great Sandy Desert, until the terrible heat and parched earth dissipates every ounce of moisture and the river simply peters out.

South of the Kimberley Plateau is one of the great wonders of the natural world. Wolf Creek Crater was formed many thousands of years ago when a huge meteorite rushed from the depths of space and plunged to earth at a speed of thousands of kilometres an hour. The terrible impact smashed a circular hole in the bedrock. The resulting crater is 854 metres across and 61 metres deep, the second largest in the world. Hundreds of kilometres to the southwest is another rock formation which draws the crowds. The Wave Rock, near Hyden, is a towering, 15 metre tall granite monolith which has been eroded by wind and water until it has assumed the shape of a gracefully curved breaker of the type loved by surfers.

But perhaps the greatest, and most famous, natural wonder of Western Australia is not as interesting as the Wolf Creek Crater, nor as beautiful as the Wave Rock. In fact it is terribly boring. What makes the Nullarbor Plain so famed is its sheer size. The flat, treeless plain stretches across more land than the entire state of Victoria and is one of the most inhospitable areas on the continent. This vast limestone plateau is riddled with caves, some of which contain remarkable natural stalactite and stalagmite formations. Across the plain runs the Trans-Australia Railway. Due to the extraordinary flatness of the region the engineers were able to lay the tracks in a straight line for 483 kilometres, the longest straight stretch of line in the world.

Another great route across the deserts of Western Australia is the 1,600 kilometre long Canning Stock Route. This track was surveyed in 1906 by A.W. Canning and for decades was used to transport cattle from Arnhem Land to the railhead at Wiluna. Modern means of transportation have long since rendered the route obsolete, the water holes have become derelict and the track difficult to follow. Even so, some specialised holiday firms organise expeditions to view the terrible heart of the Great Sandy Desert.

The more fertile areas of the state are not so abundant in mineral wealth, but they were the first to be settled by the migrants as they struggled to scratch a living from the soil. The site of the original settlement on the Swan River has long since been built over, but the type of land that Captain Stirling and his band of settlers found can be seen in many southwestern parts of the state. Sheep and wheat are the most important agricultural products in the area. Over 3 million hectares of land are given over to the production of wheat and the yield is around twenty bushels per hectare. Though the rate of production is not very high the farms are highly mechanised and farmers can enjoy a standard of living comparable to their city cousins. The sheep population of the state is around 35 million but unlike other states, wool is not the only product. Many of the sheep are bred for meat, indeed combined beef and lamb exports rival those of wool. In the northernmost areas of the state more emphasis is placed on grazing than in the southwestern part. Here farms are far larger than further south, some extending over some half million hectares or more. Unfortunately, the land is far less productive, with an average capacity of one sheep per eight hectares. In between these two relatively small, agricultural areas stretches the vast interior: the Great Sandy Desert, Great Victoria Desert and the Gibson Desert, which together with the barren hills of the west form a vast barrier to agriculture.

The great forests of the southwestern area are a vital asset of the state. Over 3 million hectares have been declared State Forests and are managed on the principle of sustained yield, thus each tree felled is replaced with another and the area of forest never diminishes. Along the coast fishing is an important money-spinner, exports of crayfish, or rock lobster, to the United States alone are worth many millions of dollars a year. Further to the north the pearling industry continues to flourish, though the pearling luggers have now been replaced by a cultured-pearl industry in Kuri Bay.

In the far southwest of the state stands the bustling capital of Perth, now the proud home of the America's Cup. The 'sunshine city' of Perth has come a long way since Captain Stirling arrived on an alien shore with his intrepid band of colonists. Today, the settlement has grown into a city throbbing with life and reflects well the prosperity of Western Australia. Indeed, the city is the hub and nerve centre of the whole state. Of the 1.3 million inhabitants of Western Australia over 900,000 live in or near their capital city. Perth is the most remote capital city in the world, being some 2,700 kilometres from Adelaide; the nearest other city of any size. Until 1976 there was only a single railway and a collection of dirt roads and tracks to connect the city with the eastern states. In that year the Eyre, or Great Eastern, Highway was completed across the Nullarbor Plain to Adelaide, and it is hoped that the Great Northern Highway to Darwin will soon be metalled.

This isolation has shaped the character and history of the city. The settlers had to be hardy and independent, able to make their own way in the world. Perth was proclaimed a city in 1856 and rapidly began to assume the role of the 'elegant city of Australia', a role it continued to play when it was made a lord mayoralty in 1929 and which persists to the present day. The city, together with the state, was largely ignored by the rest of the world, but prosperity and growth came with the discoveries of gold in the 1890s. The increasing agricultural and mineral exports which flowed through the city necessitated the improvement of Fremantle Harbour in 1901, which in turn stimulated increased exports. Today, Perth is not only accessible by road, rail and sea but also by air, via the large and impressive international airport.

Although the city is a major industrial centre, the heavy industries are concentrated in the suburbs of Fremantle, Welshpool and Kwinana. Prosperity relies on steel, aluminium and nickel; paint, plaster, cement and rubber, as well as petroleum refineries and food-processing plants.

Perth enjoys a wonderful climate. Straddling the blue waters of the Swan River – the natural habitat of the black swan – it enjoys a sea breeze which rises from Fremantle and cools the population on hot summer afternoons. The excellent climate makes all kinds of outdoor sports popular. Sailing is a passion with some people, which has resulted in the city's yacht club winning the sport's most prestigious trophy, and those not in boats can surf, swim or simply enjoy the sun and the splendid white, sandy beaches. Other favourite sports include hockey, cricket, bowls and tennis. Winter sports include "Australian Rules" football: a game with machismo. The post-war migration accounts for the existence of soccer, too. For others there is basketball, speedboat and car racing. It is all there for the taking!

The University of Western Australia is responsible for developing a mechanical sheepshearing machine, which can equal a man's time of three minutes. There is also a technical college, two teachers' training colleges and some private colleges. Perth has both Anglican and Roman Catholic cathedrals, and several historic buildings: the Barracks Arch, His Majesty's Theatre, the Town Hall with its clock tower, the Old Asylum, the Old Mill and Government House dating back to 1863.

The state of Western Australia is still 'The Frontier State'; a state of scattered homesteads, vast distances and great potential. The huge, newly-discovered deposits of minerals place Western Australia on the brink of dynamic growth, while its natural splendours and beautiful buildings truly make it 'The unique Australian state'.

Facing page in the heart of the wheat-growing belt near Hyden stand these two impressive rock formations: *top* Hippo's Yawn and *bottom* Wave Rock.

Albany *previous pages* is the oldest town in the state. The brig *Amity inset, top left* is a replica of the ship that brought the first settlers in 1826. The coastal scenery in the state's southwestern corner is spectacular: *above and right* Torndirrup National Park, *top* Cape Leeuwin and *opposite page, top* Cape Naturaliste. *Opposite page, bottom* beautiful Jewel Cave near Augusta.

Previous pages Pemberton and *insets* Manjimup. *These pages* Busselton's 2 km-long jetty *above*. Nature lies still unspoilt in the Porongorup Range *top* and Stirling Range *right* National Parks and *opposite page* near Yallingup *bottom* and Wyadup *top. Overleaf* Bunbury and *inset* its Catholic cathedral.

Previous pages can be seen Mundurah Beach. Barrack Street *left and facing page* runs along the side of the central shopping mall, as does Murray Street *above* and William Street *below*. The Mall is an area of central Perth where vehicles are prohibited and pedestrians can shop in peace and quiet. *Top left* quaint-looking London Court. *Overleaf* Perth's racecourse is to be found at Belmont Park.

Previous pages scenes in the spring of 1983 upon Alan Bond's return to Perth after winning the America's Cup (pictures by Michael Coyne/Talentbank). *Above* a gnarled tree stands watch over a park in Fremantle, Perth's port. Many of the important buildings in the city are surrounded by gardens of great beauty. *Far left* and *facing page, bottom* the neo-Gothic Catholic cathedral, which stands amid trees and shrubs in Victoria Square. *Facing page, top* the gardens that lie before the Parliament Buildings. The strange Ore Obelisk *left*, which is to be found in Stirling Gardens, was erected to mark the arrival of the millionth inhabitant of Western Australia.

Previous pages the towering business centre is an indication of the wealth which has come to Perth as a result of its booming population and industry. *Below* is a glorious example of a style of architecture little used today, as are the arches on Roe Street *left. Centre left* Forrest Place. The Carrillion Centre *facing page* is an impressive example of modern architecture put to practical use as a shopping complex. Opened in March 1983, this four-level centre cost some twenty-six million dollars. A less-inspired piece of architecture is the bus station *bottom left.*

Perth has come a long way from the collection of pioneer buildings erected by Captain Stirling in 1829. Today, the tall buildings of the business heart of the city tower above the shops and houses.

Among the parks and gardens of Perth, *bottom right* Queens Gardens and *facing page* Kings Park, many historic buildings survive from the colonial era. Turner Cottage *left* and *below* has been restored to its original condition. The Old Mill *below left* was built in the earliest days of Perth, during the 1830s, to grind the flour of the fledgling colony. Today, it is a museum and its grounds contain many interesting relics, including a mailcoach and a blacksmith's forge. *Overleaf* the towering concrete structures of modern Perth, architectural statements of the city's progress. Fluorescent light from the buildings colours the scene while the car park stands empty and forlorn.

Located in the pleasant suburb of Crawley, the University of Western Australia *these pages* is the main seat of learning for the state. Its dignified buildings, *above* and *below* Winthrop Hall, stand amid greenery. *Overleaf* the location of Perth makes watersports popular with its residents.

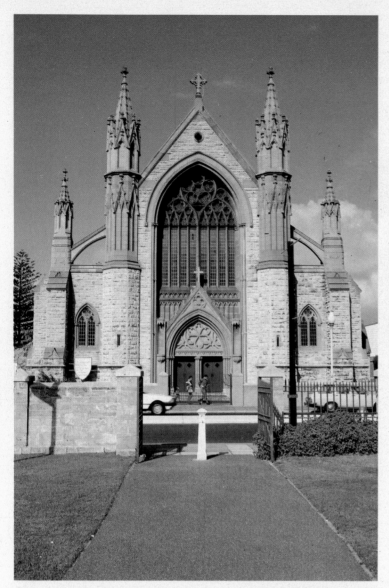

Though Fremantle *these pages* is often overshadowed by its larger neighbour, it has much to offer resident and visitor alike. The Round House Gaol *facing page, bottom,* a grim reminder of days gone by, stands alongside the High Street *facing page, top* and *left.* The magnificent buildings of the Market *far left,* the Harbour *above,* the Museum *top right* and Saint Patrick's Catholic Church *top left* are all based on European architectural styles.

Around Perth can be found many places well worth a visit. Rottnest Island *facing page, top* and *left* is a popular resort, with spectacular scenery and a charming colony of quokkas. Yanchep National Park, on the other hand, is on the mainland a few miles north of the city. It is famous for its magnificent coastal scenery *facing page, bottom,* abundance of cuddly koalas *above* and spectacular underground caves. In the fertile southwest of the state are many sheep stations, such as that near Jurien *far left.* Sheep ranching is an important aspect of the area, as is market gardening and other types of agriculture.

The southwestern corner of Western Australia is famed for the incredible beauty and diversity of its wildflowers. This is due, in part, to the varied environments of the area: the *Platytheca verticillata* *above* grows on the moist Darling Scarp, while the pink starflower *Calytrix decandra top* prefers the dry sandheaths around Esperance. *Left Kunzea parvifolia. Facing page Boronia sticta.*

The flora of Australia has been shaped by its geological history and its climate. Its original connection with the other southern continents in the supercontinent of Gondwanaland gave Australia its multitude of plant families. The recent, in geological terms, change in the continent's climate has had an equally marked effect on the plants. As the atmosphere became drier and hotter, the plants had to adapt to survive. One of the ways in which they did this was to develop small, narrow and waxy leaves that allowed for very little surface evaporation. The plants on *these pages* show this process, known as sclerosis, to perfection. *Left* scarlet honeymyrtle, *above* wiry honeymyrtle, *top right Isopognon lanenthifolia, top left Grevillea* and *facing page* the dramatic bloom of the *Beaufortia.*

These pages yellow is the dominant colour among Banksias, and is also met with in other flowers: *facing page* the *Imbertia hypericoides, above* the *Conostylis aculeata* and *right* the yellow kangaroo paw *Anigozanthus pulcherrimas*. This two-metre-tall plant is spread sparsely across the landscape north of Moora, but where it does occur it congregates in vast stands of brilliant yellow flowers. Like most kangaroo paws, this species springs from a rhizome below the soil surface and reappears each season.

While the desert flowers are almost exclusively ephemeral, springing up when it rains only to die again after producing seeds, the great beauties of the moister regions are often found on perennial shrubs. Among these magnificent blooming bushes are the *Pimelia ferruginea above*, the *Chamelaucicun uncinatum top right*, the Swan River myrtle *Hypocalymma robustum centre right* and the aptly named featherflower *Verticordia plumosa right*. This latter was the very first plant of its genus to be scientifically described and catalogued, and prefers to live on the granite outcrops of Western Australia. Like so many other flowering shrubs, it is a member of the Myrtaceae family which includes all the Eucalypts and Myrtles of Australia.

Like those of the morning iris, the flowers of the purple flag *Patersonia occidentalis above* only last for one day. Luckily, the plant has such a profusion of buds that it is covered in its 4-centimetre-wide flowers from September to November. It is by far the most common *Patersonia* in Western Australia, having a range from Esperance to beyond the Murchison River. The snakebush *Hemiandra pungens top left*, on the other hand, is to be found on the sandy coastal plain north and south of Perth. *Left* the tiny *Boronia viminea*, *facing page, top* the *Grevillea nudiflora* and *facing page, bottom Kennedia macrophylla*, a member of the Papilionaceae family.

These pages red is a vibrant colour which features strongly among the flowers of the great antipodean continent. The rose coneflower *Isopognon formous facing page* and the red pokers *Hakea bucculenta top right* both belong to the Protaceae family, which is perhaps better known as the Grevillea family. The range of this family in Australia and South Africa is a powerful clue to the previous existence of Gondwanaland, the vast southern continent of dinosaur times, which was later to divide into the continents of Africa, South America, Antarctica and Australia. The Myrtaceae family, to which belong Baxter's kunzea *Kunzea baxteri left* and the delicate murchison clawflower *Calothamnus homalophyllus top left*, is restricted to Australia and a few nearby islands. *Above* the gorgeous shades of the *Diplolaena augustifolia*.

When the British Admiralty sent a botanist along with Captain Cook on his epic voyage around the world, it intended his report to advise on the suitability of the land for agriculture. Instead, Joseph Banks came back with hundreds of dried flowers and leaves. The Admiralty may not have been impressed by this effort, but the scientific world was, and studied Banks' finds in great detail. One of the most spectacular groups of wildflowers to be found in the Australian bush has been named after this pioneer of Australian botany; the *Banksia far left*. Other beauties are the *Dryandra praemorsa left*, the *Calothamnus homalophyllus bottom left*, the *Grevillea bipinnatifida bottom right* and the *Verticordia serrat facing page*.

The Aizoaceae family is very rarely seen on the continent of Australia, but it counts among its members some of the loveliest flowers of the outback; the delicate coastal pigface *facing page*, for example. The orchid family, on the other hand, is very common on the continent, the donkey orchid *right* being a widespread species. *Above* the *Calothamnus gilesii* and the flame tree *top* are just two of the vast number of red blooms that decorate the countryside.

York *these pages* is the oldest inland town in the state, dating from 1830.

Its main street is lined with an impressive array of historic buildings.

The great gold cities of Western Australia, Coolgardie and Kalgoorlie, both commemorate their pioneers in street names. The building seen *right* stands on Coolgardie's Bayley Street.

It was Arthur Bayley and his friend William Ford who discovered gold here. Kalgoorlie named its main street *remaining pictures* after Paddy Hannan, who stumbled across the Golden Mile.

Unlike most other towns of the Gold Rush days, Kalgoorlie has survived into the late twentieth century with a promising future. Over a thousand tonnes of gold have been wrested from the earth in this area, and it is still being found. Many of the grandest buildings in the city date from the boom days; the Town Hall *above* was built in 1908. Another great feature of the old

times is the pipeline that runs a staggering 597 kilometres from Perth to provide the thirsty miners with water. The peak population of 30,000 has now fallen to some 20,000, but the city is now an established centre. Gold mining continues, of course, but the pastoral potential of the surrounding countryside is now being realised. *Overleaf* the Pinnacles.

The area of land some hundred miles north of Perth is among the loveliest in the whole state. The views of the sheep station inland from Jurien *opposite page, top* and Cervantes Beach *opposite page, bottom* are typical. Jurien is a major lobster catching centre, an importance belied by its population of just 600. Salvado College *right* and *above* is to be found in the town of New Norcia, whose church is shown *top* and hotel *centre right*. The college caters for students from all over the state. The town has its origins in a Spanish Benedictine Mission founded in 1846 to help the local Aborigines. The gracious buildings stand in the dusty Moore Valley where sheep and wheat are important products.

Geraldton *this page* with St Francis Xavier Cathedral *top left* is a major port for the mid-west region.

Port Hedland is 1,000 km further north along outback roads *opposite, bottom* and exports salt *opposite, top*.

These pages Kalbarri National Park lies some 150 km north of Geraldton and is noted for its coloured rock cliffs, the banded appearance of which is due to beds of red sandstone that underlie the region.

Over thousands of years, the whole coastal plain has been uplifted by some 200 metres, creating the inland gorges and coastal cliffs. The Murchison River has cut a canyon through the area, known as 'The Loop'.

Previous pages the beach near Kalbarri. The Hamersley Range *these pages and overleaf* stands at the heart of the mineral-rich Pilbara. Throughout the area towns, such as Tom Price and Paraburdoo, exist as bases for the iron ore mining. Thousands of tons of rock are ripped from the ground each year and loaded on giant trains for transport to the coast. But the region's chief attraction for tourists is its remarkable scenery. Plunging chasms drop hundreds of metres to almost dry river beds. Tinto Gorge *below left* is a striking example. But most dramatic of all are the colours: vivid hues of red and mauve, interspersed with the golden bands of dry spinifex, paint the canyon walls and draw thousands of tourists here each year.

These pages within Hamersley Ranges National Park, Western Australia. It contains a series of high and rugged mountains, spectacular gorges, waterfalls and pools. *Facing page, top* Circular Pool, Dale's Gorge. *Facing page, bottom* Dale's Gorge Lookout. The walls of the gorges rise sheer out of the still, cool waters and, beneath the noonday sun, the rocks can glow to seeming incandescence within the flaming furnace of this dry land.

Broome *these pages* on the Great Northern Highway was, at the turn of the century, a rip-roaring pearling port. *Overleaf* landscape near Kununurra.

Kununurra *previous pages,*
above and opposite page,
top is the centre for a
vast irrigation project
centred on the Ord River.
The dam *opposite page,*
bottom created Australia's
largest artificial lake;
Lake Argyle *overleaf. Page*
96 the perennial
strawflower *Helichrysum*
bracteatum.